To Mom,
for all the
love, worry, and laughter

*"All that I am, or hope to be,
I owe to my angel mother."*

- Abraham Lincoln

Table of Contents

Table of Contents

Acknowledgements

The author gratefully acknowledges the help, kindness, and guidance from:

Ted Inoué
Brett Nielsen
Susan Korman
Christopher Mott
Kajikawa Family
Gary and Mari Gentel
Gary Gand
Annamarie Pileggi
Steven and Danielle Baughn
Eyoälha Baker – Jump for Joy Photo Project
Robert Grozalis (Synergy Hearing)
Michael Gardner
Dan Birdwell
Luciana
Girl Scouts of America
Philadelphia Eagles

Preface

Several years ago, I began to notice that everywhere I went with my mom, Kimiko, people smiled and laughed. There is a random wackiness about her that makes people remember and look forward to seeing her again.

It is amazing how my mom maintained her sense of humor throughout her ninety years. She was born in 1929 in Tokyo, Japan. During World War II, her family of seven had little food to eat. Even though she was a young girl, my mom was the only person in her family that wasn't too proud to beg. She spent every day foraging for food and bringing it home to feed her family. Her brother credits her for saving their lives.

As a fifteen-year-old, my mom survived the Bombing of Tokyo on March 9-10, 1945. It left an estimated 100,000 civilians dead and over one million people homeless when the United States firebombed the city. It is regarded as the single most destructive bombing raid in human history. To this day, my mom cannot talk about it. Nine of her family members were killed, and, sadly, many more of her family and friends died during World War II.

Despite so much suffering and tragedy, it's extraordinary how she has maintained her sense of humor. After a lifetime of watching my mom make others laugh, I realized how meaningful it would be to capture her whimsical spirit.

When I started sharing her anecdotes with friends, I was overwhelmed by the positive response. Friends asked to hear more "Mom stories" and encouraged me to compile them into a book. *My Wacky Mom: Wacky Wisdom of the Ages* is the result of their encouragement.

It is truly my hope that my blessed mom's whimsical spirit brings you laughter and levity.

Evy Inoué

*"If God had meant us to walk around naked,
he would never have invented the wicker chair."*

- Erma Bombeck (humorist)

Chapter 1:

Love, Nudity, & Sex

My Wacky Mom on Low IQ Men

Mom: "Low IQ men are better. Much better than high IQ men. If I got married, I'd rather marry a low IQ man. HE WILL OBEY ME! Not a homely one. A good-looking guy."

Me: "Are you serious?"

Mom: "You don't know. They obey. They are like puppy dogs."

Me: "How do you know?"

Mom: "There's a guy who works at my building. He's really nice. He has a smartphone. He drives. His wife calls to check up on him. He obeys her. Whatever his wife says, he does."

Me: "That's what you want?"

Mom: "Better than some smart lazy bum. He's hard-working. One time, I gave him $5 for helping me. He really appreciated it even though he can't write me a thank you note."

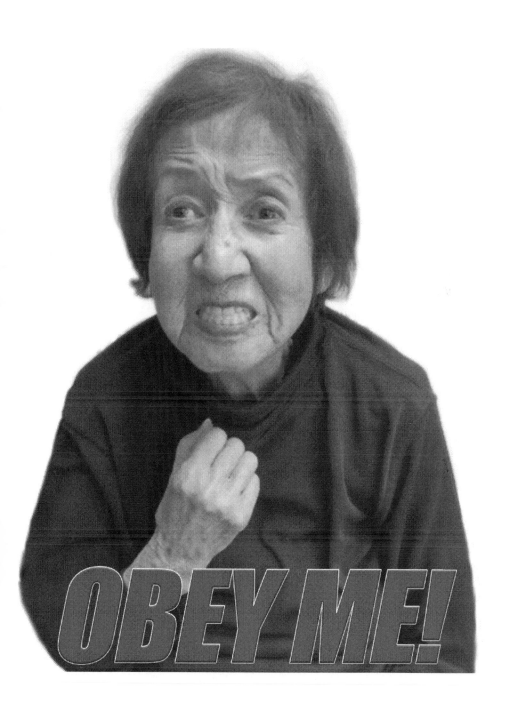

My Wacky Mom on Chinese Men

Mom: "I love looking at the new Asian drama catalog!"

Me: "What Asian drama do you like?"

Mom: "Drama with good-looking Chinese guys. I'm not interested in watching ugly guys. I like them young. I just look. I don't need to touch."

Me: "Wow! What else do you like?"

Mom: "I really like it when guys go in the pool -- guys with real nice figures. This one actor, he's got a real good-looking face, but he never takes off his clothes. I'm pretty sure he has skinny legs."

Me: (chuckling)

Mom: "Stop laughing! What else do I have?"

My Wacky Mom on Nudity

Mom: "Help!"

Me: "What's wrong?"

Mom: "My friend gave me a cookie. I cut it into four pieces and ate three of them. But one piece is missing! It's driving me crazy! I took off all my clothes and still can't find it. What should I do?"

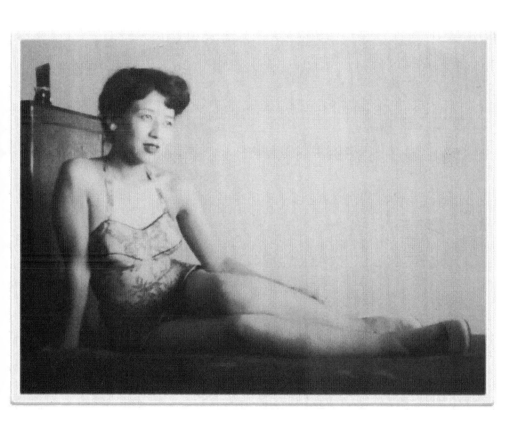

My Wacky Mom on Male News Anchors

Mom: "What happened to the guy on Channel 3?"

Me: "What guy?"

Mom: "The news guy. I think his name is Jeff."

Me: "How would I know? You know I don't watch the news."

Mom: "He's a good-looking guy. Around forty years old. What happened to him? Did he have sex?"

Me: "What?"

Me: "You know those news guys. They have sex and then they disappear."

My Wacky Mom in a Love Triangle

My Mom's Apartment Manager (calling me): "There's been a complaint lodged against your mom."

Me: "What?"

Manager: "A resident's wife is complaining that your mom is having a romantic relationship with her husband."

Me: "No way."

Manager: "Your mom has gone up to this man's wife on three different occasions saying, 'I love your husband.'"

Me: "My mom???"

Manager: "I investigated. I found out that the man, Ed, and your mom have a mutual passion for the 'Free Table.' They show up on Fridays and find free things on the table for each other. Ed was a merchant seaman in Japan, so when your mom and he see each other at the Free Table, they bow to one another and start rummaging."

Me: "Should I talk to my mom?"

Manager: "No. I handled it. I told Ed's wife not to worry. Your mom has no interest whatsoever in romantic relationships. She just likes free things."

My Wacky Mom on How to "Do Sex"

Mom: "I need you to cancel my doctor's appointment."

Me: "Why? Don't you need to see the urologist?"

Mom: "I don't ever want to go back there. The office is covered with signs that tell people how to 'do sex.' I don't need that!"

Me: "Are you sure?"

Mom (nods): "Mama mia! Yes, I am sure!"

Never Too Old For Safe Sex

Practice Safe Sex:

- ❖ Talk to your doctor
- ❖ Use condoms
- ❖ Get tested for Sexually Transmitted Diseases

My Wacky Mom On Keith Urban

Mom (suddenly looking very serious): "Don't laugh at me. I need your help. I want to buy Keith Urban."

My Wacky Mom on Arranged Marriages

Mom: "When your grandmother was twenty-six years old, her parents said she needed to get married right away. She was getting too 'old' for marriage. She was really good-looking and in love with a guy who had eight brothers and sisters. Her parents wouldn't let her marry the guy because she would have to move into the family home, and his family was too big."

Me: "So, what happened?"

Mom: "My mother was very angry. She told her parents, 'I don't care. I'll just marry the ugly guy, but I won't ever look at his face.' So, she married the ugly guy -- your grandfather."

Me: "So, when did she look at his face?"

Mom: "She never looked at his face. Too ugly."

"You have to play this game like somebody just hit your mother with a two-by-four."

- Dan Birdwell (#53, former defensive lineman, Oakland Raiders)

Chapter 2:

Football

My Wacky Mom on Becoming a Football Fan in her Eighties

Mom: "I love football!"

Me: "What happened? My entire life you've hated sports. Why did you become a football fan in your eighties?"

Mom: "I love to watch good-looking guys with nice figures sweat and run around."

Me: It's all about good-looking guys?"

Mom: "That's only part of it! I spend a lot of time studying about football and the players. I read about their lives, too. It makes me happy. When I watch football, I scream, I cheer, and I cry tears of joy."

Me: "I'd love to watch a game with you sometime."

Mom: "No way, José! I like to watch football alone. That way, I can eat and go to the bathroom whenever I want."

My Wacky Mom on Gloating

Me: "How was the Eagles game?"

Mom: "It was fantastic! I'm really lucky! My team won! I'm the lucky one! So good!"

Me: "That's terrific."

Mom: "Before the game, my neighbor, Bob, said to me, 'Kimiko, there is NO WAY the Eagles are gonna win.' So, after the game, I wrote Bob a letter and hung it on his door. I even drew a picture of a funny man laughing. I wrote: 'Dear Bob, I cannot believe it! Ha-ha-ha! You were wrong! I am right! The Eagles won!'"

My Wacky Mom on When the Philadelphia Eagles Lose

Mom: "That was the most terrible football game I ever saw. This is not football. Throw the ball a short distance. Catch it. Don't give the ball to anyone else. Terrible! Terrible! Stinks! Stinks! Stink! Stink! If I was healthy, I could do this!"

Me: "What would you do?"

Mom: "I would get more guys that are 7' 3" with big bodies. Guys that sweat a lot and drink water all the time. Those kind of guys make the best football players."

Me: "That would make the game better!"

Mom: "Right? Today's game was no fun. So boring! I was so mad. I didn't want to watch football anymore. So, I changed the channel and watched absolutely gorgeous Chinese men instead."

My Wacky Mom on Dolling Up for the Super Bowl

Mom: "My apartment building is having a Philadelphia Eagles party today. I'm all ready for the Super Bowl!"

Me: "What did you do to get ready?"

Mom: "I am wearing my Eagles hat, Eagles scarf, Eagles sweatshirt, and Eagles socks! I even painted my nails green!"

Me: "Wow!"

Mom: "I practiced how to sing the Eagles song, too." **(singing)**

♬ "Fly, Eagles Fly! ♬

♬ On the road to victory! ♬

My Wacky Mom on the Philadelphia Eagles Winning Super Bowl LII

Mom: "I can't believe it. The Eagles won the Super Bowl! I am so happy! My tears are coming out!"

Me: "Congratulations! You're making me cry, too."

Mom: "I thought I was going to die watching the game. Now that the Eagles won, I am surrounded by fireworks. My apartment sounds like it's going to explode! Everybody is so happy!"

Me: "That is incredible!"

Mom: "This is the most exciting thing that has ever happened to me! I don't have any time to talk to you. Don't bother me for at least a few days." **(dial tone)**

*"Fell asleep with my breast pump on,
and I think I'm in a different dimension now."*

- Chrissy Teigen (model, author)

Chapter 3:

Entertainment & Technology

My Wacky Mom on Getting to Know the Cable Guy

Mom: "The cable guy just left. He was really nice."

Me: "Did he fix your TV?"

Mom: "Yes, it works great. We had a lot of fun."

Me: "Fun?"

Mom: "After he fixed my TV, I got out my karaoke. I sang for him. Then, he sang a song for me.

My Wacky Mom on Her Streaming Device, the Roku

Mom: "I'm so exhausted. I was going to watch Chinese raccoon, but my raccoon won't move."

Me: "What are you talking about?"

Mom: "I have so many gizmos here. My remote control works but my raccoon doesn't move."

Me: "Are you talking about your Roku?"

Mom: "Yes! Mama mia!"

Me: "Did you change the battery?"

Mom: "Hold on! **(changes battery)** My raccoon works!"

My Wacky Mom on Jerry Springer

Mom: "I watch this TV show. I love it. Strippers come down a pole. They fight all the time and beat each other up."

Me: "You like to watch strippers?"

Mom: "I would much rather watch this stupid show than something that makes me depressed. I can watch three hours at a time. It's so funny. It makes me laugh."

Me: "Are you watching *Jerry Springer*?"

Mom: "YES! That's the show! I love it!"

My Wacky Mom on Her "New" CD Player

Mom: "There's something wrong with this CD player. I can't hear it. The sound quality is really, really bad."

Me (trying it out): "It sounds okay to me."

Mom: "What do you know? You don't listen to CDs. I know the difference. It is the lowest quality. You must return it."

Me: "Try it again."

Mom (looking extremely skeptical but tries again): "Now, I can hear it. What did you do?"

Me: "I turned up the volume."

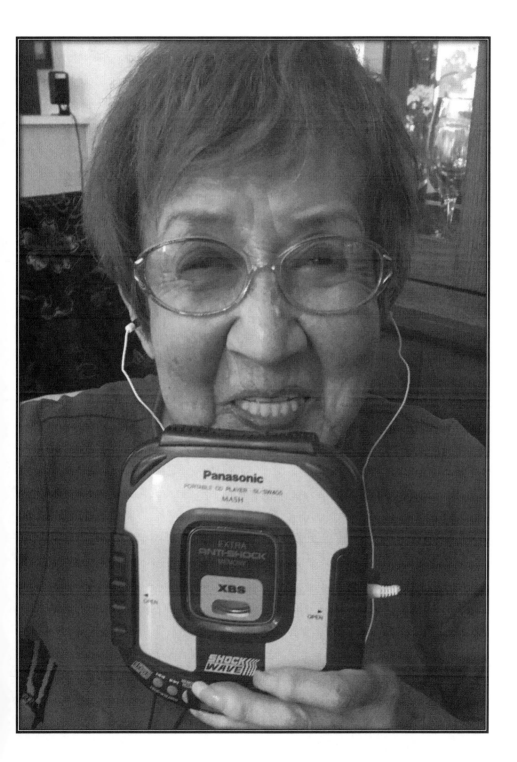

My Wacky Mom on Dinner Theaters

Mom: "That dinner theater was terrible. I hated it!"

Me: "Why was it terrible?"

Mom: "My biggest memory of the day was when I got STUCK IN THE TOILET. I couldn't open the bathroom door. I was terrified and screamed my head off. Janice flipped on her back and slid on the bathroom floor and got me out of the toilet!"

Postscript:

I called Janice to thank her for her daring rescue. I said, "Thank you for going beyond the call of duty -- literally." Janice responded, "To be honest, I just wanted your mom to stop screaming bloody murder."

My Wacky Mom on Phone Sex

Mom: "Every day they call. Two or three sperms. They don't leave a message. I guess they want to talk to me. I think they want to 'do sex' or something."

Me: "Did you say sperm?"

Mom: "Yes. What is this sperm? I get so many phone calls. Every single day. They all say 'Sperm something.'"

Me: "Do you mean spam?"

Mom: "Yes. This sperm talks a long time. Going to give me a trip to Florida. Give me money."

Me: "Can you write down the phone number that calls you, so I can tell them to stop calling?"

Mom: "No way! I'm not going to get up every time this sperm calls. Gotta watch Chinese men!" **(dial tone)**

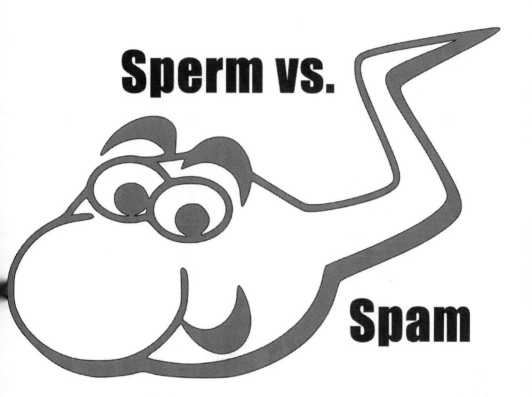

Sperm vs.

Spam

"I may be a senior, but so what? I'm still hot!"

- Betty White (b. 1922) with Luciana in music video, "I'm Still Hot"

Chapter 4:

Health & Aging

My Wacky Mom on Being Prepared

Mom: "I'm so happy! I just got a business card from a guy who says that HE WILL TAKE EVERYTHING WHEN I DIE!"

Me: "What?"

Mom: "You won't have to worry about emptying out my apartment. He will take everything as soon as I die. Hold on. I will give you his phone number."

Me: "You're not going to die tonight, are you?"

Mom: "It would be really nice to die in the middle of the night. Call him now!"

My Wacky Mom on Preparing for a Blood Test

Mom: "You told me that I couldn't eat or drink anything after 9 pm for my blood test tomorrow. I don't trust myself to remember, so do you know what I did?"

Me: "No. What did you do?"

Mom: "I took my really big tape, and I taped up my whole refrigerator so I wouldn't eat or drink anything."

Me: "You're kidding, right?"

Mom: "Why would I kid you? I taped the top and the bottom of the refrigerator. Then, I made a sign. Guess what?! It worked! I didn't eat or drink anything all night long!"

My Wacky Mom on Vanity

Mom: "Do you remember the lady that works at my building, Sue?"

Me: "Yes."

Mom: "Sue is sixty-five years old. She wears a wig and never takes it off. She glues it on her head and even sleeps with it on her head."

Me (chuckles): "How can she do that?"

Mom: "This is not funny. Everything needs fresh air. She doesn't have any teeth, either."

Me: "Does she wear her teeth to bed, too?"

Mom: "No, I'm pretty sure she doesn't."

Me: "How do you know?"

Mom: "One time she came to work without her teeth."

Me: "Really?"

Mom: "She held a scarf over her mouth all day. Sue said to me, 'I tell people I have a cold when I actually just forgot to put in my teeth.'"

My Wacky Mom on Hemorrhoids

Mom: "Did you know that my mother's side of the family all have bad hemorrhoids?"

Me: "No, I didn't."

Mom: "That's why my cousin changed his name."

Me: "Your cousin changed his name because he had bad hemorrhoids?"

Mom: "When my cousin was a child, he was sick all the time. His doctors suggested that my aunt and uncle change his name, so he wouldn't get hemorrhoids."

Me: "Did it help?"

Mom: "No."

My Wacky Mom on Doctors' Nicknames

About five years ago, my mom began her tradition of calling doctors by their specialty. It all started with her neurologist, Dr. Wolf. My mom always called him, "Dr. Brain."

Fortunately Dr. Brain was a very patient man. Here is photographic evidence that my mom now names all her doctors after the appropriate body part.

I am quite relieved that she no longer goes to the gynecologist!

SUNDAY	MONDAY	TUESDAY	WEDNESDAY	THURSDAY	FRIDAY	SATURDAY
					1 DR. FOOT 10=30	2
3	4	5 ● Chinese New Year	6	7	8	9
10	11 DR. Brain 1:15	12 ☽	13	14 Valentine's Day	15 DR. Ear 11:30 National Flag Day (Canada)	16
17	18	19 ○	20	21	22	23

61

My Wacky Mom on the 600-Year-Old Pope

Mom: "Did you hear that the pope is retiring?"

Me: "No."

Mom: "He's 600-years-old."

Me: "That's impossible. He's younger than you."

Mom: "No way, José! I'm not 600-years-old! I'm 69 plus!"

My Wacky Mom on Helping Her Helper

Mom: "My aide is eighty-years-old. She looks like she could be my mother."

Me: "What?! I can't believe they gave you an eighty-year-old aide!"

Mom: "She doesn't walk so well. I won't ask her to vacuum."

Me: "What do you mean?"

Mom: "I'd rather vacuum. This lady might fall over and knock down my TV. I can't survive without my TV!"

Me: "You survived World War II. Of course you would survive without a TV."

Me: "Are you kidding? I need a TV! What else do I have? Help!"

"The most remarkable thing about my mother is that for thirty years she served the family nothing but leftovers. The original meal has never been found."

- Calvin Trillin (author, humorist)

Chapter 5:

Religion, Holidays & Celebrations

My Wacky Mom on Memorial Day

Mom: "Marianne, the lady who lives in the apartment above me, died on Memorial Day."

Me: "Oh no! What happened?"

Mom: "Marianne was ninety-two years old. Her family was visiting for the holiday, and they were talking in the living room. Marianne dropped dead right in the middle of her sentence."

Me: "That's terrible."

Mom: "Terrible? It is wonderful! What a great way to die. Marianne is so lucky!"

My Wacky Mom on Ash Wednesday

Mom: "Since the President of Controlling Old Ladies kicked me out of bingo, I decided to try church instead."

Me: "How did you 'try church?'"

Mom: "The church sent me a letter. They said they would come over to my place on Ash Wednesday. So, I signed up, and they came to my apartment."

Me: "What did they do?"

Mom: "They showed up and put black stuff on my face. Then, when I went to wash my face, my whole face turned black."

My Wacky Mom on Watching Parades

Mom: "I don't know if I want to watch parades anymore."

Me: "Why?"

Mom: "I start crying."

Me: "Why do you cry?"

Mom: "So many young people dancing with no coats on."

My Wacky Mom on Turning 88 (Rice age - Beiju)

In Japan, happiness is making it to your 88th birthday (Rice Age - Beiju). The 88th birthday is considered the luckiest birthday of all.

Today is a very special day. It is my mom's 88th birthday. She is now "rice age," a most happy and joyous occasion.

It is called "rice age" because the character for rice, 米, looks like the characters for eight tens plus eight (八十八). Rice is fundamental in Japan and symbolizes purity and goodness.

Happy 88th Birthday, Mom!

My Wacky Mom on Holiday Parties

Mom: "I don't want to go to any parties."

Me: "Why?"

Mom: "Lots of idiots."

My Wacky Mom on Jehovah's Witnesses

Mom: "One of my friends is a Jehovah's Witness. I wish I could be like her."

Me: "Why?"

Mom: "Jehovah's Witnesses believe that every day is Christmas. It would be nice if every day was Christmas."

Me: "Jehovah's Witnesses don't believe in Christmas at all."

Mom: "Whatever."

My Wacky Mom on Christmas

Me (on phone): "Merry Christmas, Mom!"

Mom: "I'm busy. I'm eating."

Me: "You don't have time to wish your daughter a Merry Christmas?"

Mom: (dial tone)

"I wonder how often my kids look at me & think, 'This bitch is crazy!'"

- Anonymous

Chapter 6:

Etiquette And

Relationships

My Wacky Mom on Four-Letter Words

Me: "Hi, Mom! I'm calling to remind you of your visit this morning with the social worker."

Mom: "Yes, the lady's name is 'Damn King.'"

Me: "Who? How do you spell her name?"

Mom: "*D-a-m-n . . . K-i-n-g.* That sounds funny, doesn't it? I'm pretty sure I need to put an '*I*' in front of her name, 'I Damn King.' Is that right?"

Me (laughing so hard, I can barely speak): "Her name is Tina King."

My Wacky Mom on Heartfelt Apologies

Mom: "I apologized to that stinking old lady."

Me: "What did you say?"

Mom: "I'm sorry. I didn't mean to..."

Me: "You didn't mean to what?"

Mom: "I forgot already. I don't care. That lady is a stupid idiot!"

My Wacky Mom on Forgiveness

Mom: "When I was a kid, I was a troublemaker."

Me: "Really? What did you do?"

Mom: "One of my classmates didn't know how to add 7 plus 3. So, I called her '7 plus 3 girl.' I would follow her around the class all the time singing, '7 plus 3 girl doesn't know the answer. 7 plus 3 girl, you cannot answer.'"

Me: "That wasn't nice."

Mom: "I know. I was an idiot. But when I went back to Japan twenty-five years later, I tried to visit her at her house."

Me: "What happened?"

Mom: "She refused to see me."

Me: "You actually thought she'd be happy to see you?"

Mom: "Yes."

My Wacky Mom on Random Acts of Kindness

Mom: "The mailman stopped by my apartment. He said he had fifty-five books about Japan. He thought I would like them."

Me: "Did you take them?"

Mom: "'No way!' I told him, 'Those books are old and brown. They stink. They smell like basement.'"

Me: "I guess he won't be coming back..."

My Wacky Mom on How to Write a Thank You Note

My Wacky mom wrote me this thank you note -- for CASH!

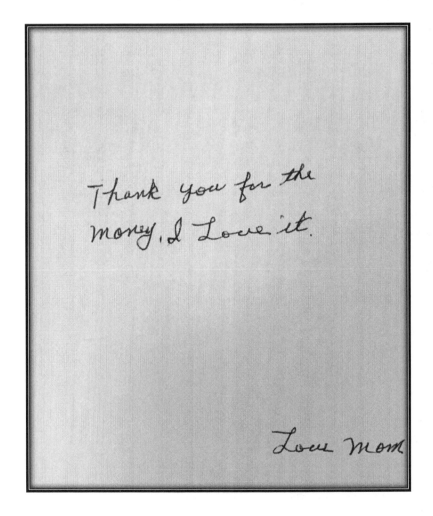

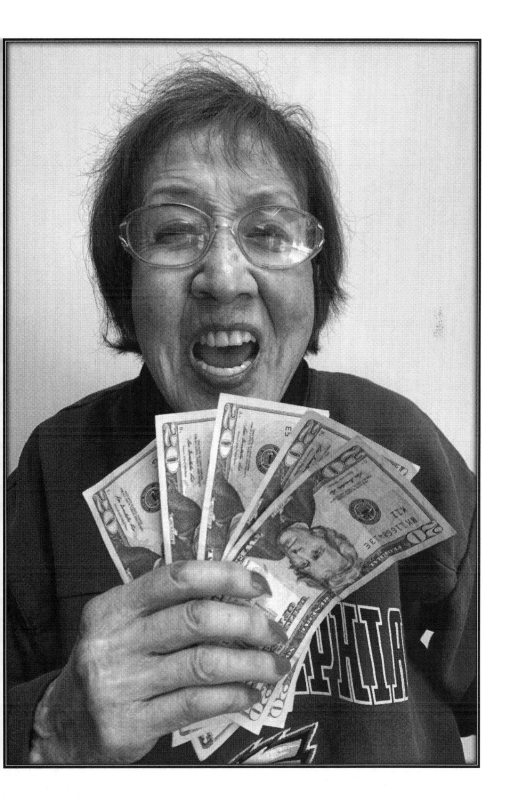

My Wacky Mom On How to Say Things In a Nice Way

Mom: "I don't like the way my aide smells -- especially her jacket. I can't stand it when she puts her jacket on my couch. I won't let her put her jacket on my couch."

Me: "Really? How do you tell her?"

Mom: "Oh. I say it in a nice way. I tell her, 'You don't mind. I don't like that you put your jacket on my couch. Put your coat on a hanger and hang it my bathroom.'"

Me: "No way! She actually hangs her coat in your bathroom?"

Mom: "Yes, then it's a little bit better. I don't have to smell it."

My Wacky Mom on Greeting Cards

Mom: "A lady who works at my apartment building has been sick for a while. She just came back. A lot of people are giving her cards. Do you have a 'Welcome Home' card I can give her?"

Me: "It's not her home. It's her work."

Mom: "Oh good. I won't bother giving her a card then."

"Mother told me a couple of years ago, 'Sweetheart, settle down and marry a rich man.' I said, 'Mom, I am a rich man.'"

- Cher (musician, actress)

Chapter 7:

Lost in Translation

My Wacky Mom on the 100-Year-Old Cat

Mom: "My friend's cat is the oldest cat that has ever lived. It is MORE than a 100 years-old."

Me: "That's impossible."

Mom: "You don't know."

Me (checking *Guinness World Records*): "The oldest cat that ever lived was 38 years old. His name was Creme Puff, and he was from Austin, Texas."

Mom: "But Sumiko's cat is older. It is over 100 years old."

Me (calling Sumiko on speakerphone): "How old is your cat?"

Sumiko: "Twenty-two years old."

Mom: "Whatever."

My Wacky Mom on Grocery Shopping

Me: "It's so hot today, Mom. You'd better stay home. Do you need anything from the grocery store?"

Mom: "I need sugar. Don't get the big bags."

Me: "Okay. What size do you want?"

Mom: "The really small sugars are 32 pounds each. Get me two of them."

My Wacky Mom on Identical Twins

Mom: "Your dogs are so cute. Are they identical twins?"

Me: "Uh, no..."

My Wacky Mom's BFF on Subtitles

Mom: "Can you believe that Sumiko is going to be on TV?"

Me: "Really? What for?"

Mom: "She's on a show about grandmothers from different countries who are all really good cooks like Sumiko."

Me: "That's exciting! I can't wait to watch it."

Mom: "They sent Sumiko the tape of her show, so she could see it before anyone else. Sumiko was insulted."

Me: "Insulted? Why?"

Mom: "Sumiko said, 'Out of all the shows, I'm the only grandmother with subtitles.' But, after Sumiko thought about it, she laughed and said, 'It's okay. Even my own kids don't know what I'm saying.'"

"Friends, Romans, Countrymen, lend me your ears."

- Mark Antony (Roman politician & general, 83-30 BC)

Chapter 8:

Say What?

My Wacky Mom at the Audiologist

Doctor: "How are your ears doing?"

Mom: "What?"

Doctor: "You're used to saying that."

Mom: "What?"

Doctor: "I'm going to look in your ears."

Mom: "What?"

Doctor: "Now say something."

Mom: "I wish I could kill myself."

Doctor: "You're pretty happy most of the time."

Mom: "I have a TV. I still drive. I'm not so interesting. Hurry up! Are you done?"

My Wacky Mom on Dollar Stores

Mom: "Did you know that you can get your nails done cheap at the Dollar Store?"

Me: "Where did you hear that?"

Mom: "A lady who lives in my building has really nice nails. I asked her where she goes. She told me the Dollar Store."

Me: "I don't think you heard her right."

Mom: "What?"

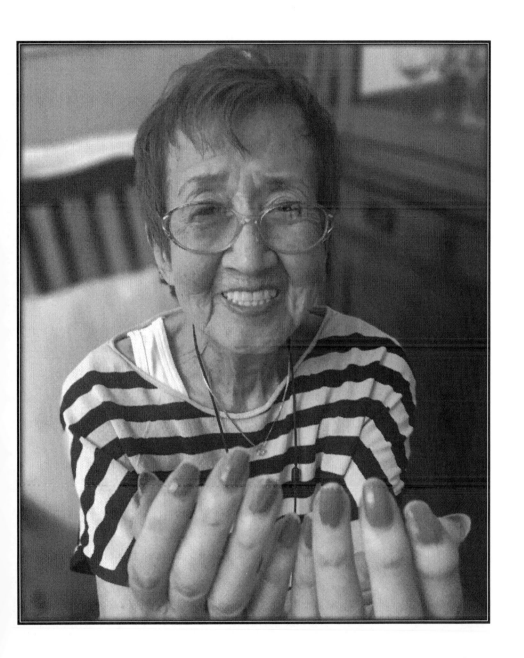

My Wacky Mom on B-I-N-G-O

Mom: "I got kicked out of bingo."

Me: "Really? What happened?"

Mom: "I never played bingo before. My friend was telling me how to play. She was talking loud, since I can't hear. The other people got really annoyed. So they reported me to the President."

Me: "The President? The President of what?"

Mom: "The President of Controlling Old Ladies."

My Wacky Mom on Distrust

Mom (calls me): "Hello."

Me (answering phone): "Hi, Mom."

Mom: "Who is this?"

Me: "This is your daughter, Evelyn. You just called me. Who do you think it is?"

Mom: "I don't believe you. You don't sound like my daughter."

Me: "You woke me up. I haven't spoken to anyone yet. That is why my voice sounds a little different."

Mom: "I have something important to say, but I can't tell you. You are not my daughter."

Me: "I will prove that I am your daughter. Ask me a question that only your daughter could answer, and then you will know that it is me."

Mom: "No. I won't do that. I don't know who you are."

Me: "My father's name is Bill."

Mom: "I'm going to hang up now whoever you are. I'm calling my daughter." **(dial tone)**

My Wacky Mom on Drag Queens

Mom: "I want to see your bingo pictures."

Me: "Oh good. You're going to love them! They are really funny."

Mom: "What kind of bingo is this?"

Me: "Country bingo. We had country music and a hoedown."

Mom (laughing and pointing at photo): "Is this person a he or a she?"

Me: "He's a drag queen."

Mom: "He owns a dry cleaner?"

My Wacky Mom on Robbing Banks

Mom: "Hey, Dr. Ear! I can't wait to get my new hearing aid."

Doctor (puts in hearing aid): "I think you will be very satisfied."

Mom: "Wow! I can hear everything! I can hear so well that I could rob a bank!"

Doctor: "That's something else!"

Mom: "WHAT?! What did you say? Hearing is not that important. But, if I can't see, I will shoot myself."

Doctor: "You wouldn't want to do that."

Mom: "You wouldn't know, Doctor! Can I leave now? I need air. I need to be free."

"My mom said the only reason men are alive is for lawn care and vehicle maintenance."

- Tim Allen (actor & comedian)

Chapter 9:

Car Trouble

My Wacky Mom on Beep, Beep, Beep

Mom: "Today I heard a *beep, beep, beep* noise. I didn't know what it was, so I drove the car to my mechanic."

Me: "What happened?"

Mom: "I yelled, 'Help! Help me! What's wrong with my car? It's making this funny noise.'"

Me: "What did he say?"

Mom: "He stuck his head in my car, laughed, and said, 'You aren't wearing your seat belt.'"

My Wacky Mom on Becoming the Incredible Shrinking Woman

Mom: "I think my legs are getting shorter. I don't know what to do!"

Me: "What makes you think that?"

Mom: "I can't reach the pedals in my car anymore. I'm shrinking!"

Me (gets in and out of her car): "Try it now."

Mom (gets in car): "Wow! My feet reach the pedals. I can't believe it. I'm not getting shorter! My legs aren't shrinking! What did you do?"

Me: "I moved your car seat forward."

My Wacky Mom on Batman

Mom: "It took me over two hours to get home from your house."

Me: "Oh no! What happened?"

Mom: "I got stuck behind a parade. Batman knocked on my window. I was terrified. He told me that I would have to turn around."

Me: "Batman knocked on your window?"

Mom: "Yes. I told him, "I am not good at backing up my car."

Me: "Why didn't you ask Batman to back up your car?"

Mom: "Batman had on a mask and a costume, so he couldn't drive a car. So, Batman told me that I would have to wait a couple of hours. He was very nice."

My Wacky Mom on Getting to the Mechanic

Mom: "I'm having car problems."

Me: "What's wrong?"

Mom: "My car doesn't always start."

Me: "Should I make an appointment for you?"

Mom: "No. I already made one. I asked my friend to drive me to the garage if my car doesn't start."

Me: "How will that help?"

Mom: "I told you. My friend could take me to the garage."

Me: "What will the mechanic be able to do with you but not your car?"

Mom (laughs): "Whatever."

My Wacky Mom on Potholes

Mom: "The police stopped me!"

Me: "What happened?"

Mom: "The cop used his siren and made lots of noise, but I didn't hear him. He came real close to me. He said he was after me for a long time."

Me: "Why did he stop you?"

Mom: "He said, 'I am really concerned about the way you drive. You were all over the road. You are going to have an accident.'"

Me: "Oh no!"

Mom: "I told him, 'There are potholes all over the road. I was driving around them!'"

Me: "Did he give you a ticket?"

Mom: "No. He said, 'I'm going to call your daughter.' Did he call you?"

Me: "No."

Mom: "I was shaking like crazy! My heart was beating so bad. I asked him if I should just drive straight over the big potholes? I was afraid to do anything. He told me to just go."

Me: "I'm so sorry."

Mom: "When you drive, do you just ignore the big potholes and drive right through them and get big holes in your tires?"

Me: "No. I try to go around potholes."

Mom: "How come the police don't come after you? I'm trouble, I tell you!"

"Mothers are all slightly insane."

- J.D. Salinger (author)

Chapter 10:

Witticisms

My Wacky Mom on Stakeouts

Mom: "I'm so mad!"

Me: "Why?"

Mom: "One of the guys in my building is an idiot. He won't wait for a washing machine. So, he goes to the laundry room, takes people's laundry out of the machines, and tosses their laundry in the garbage! I decided to stake the laundry room to catch him in the act."

Me: "Did it work?"

Mom: "Yes. I caught him removing laundry from Washing Machine #1 and Washing Machine #2 and throwing the laundry in the garbage."

Me: "Oh my gosh! Did you report him to the manager?"

Mom: "No way, José! That laundry thief is crazy. He's even crazier than me!"

My Wacky Mom on "Bookstore Kimi-chan"

Mom: "I was such a troublemaker when I was a kid. When kids played house, they never wanted to play with me."

Me: "Why?"

Mom: "My friends would play all the different family: baby, father, sisters, brothers. Not me! I ALWAYS had to play the part of Mom. If the other kids asked to play Mom, I would get very angry and yell, 'If I can't be Mom, I will kill you!' So, the other kids said, 'Watch out for 'Bookstore Kimi-chan!'"

Me: "Bookstore Kimi-chan? They called you that because your dad owned a bookstore?"

Mom: "Yes, and because everyone had to OBEY ME! Everyone was terrified of Bookstore Kimi-chan!"

My Wacky Mom on Geography

Mom: "If you go to Alaska, you'll need a passport."

Me: "I don't think so…"

Mom: "Don't you know that Alaska is part of Russia? It is not part of the United States!"

Me: "Alaska is one of the fifty states."

Mom: "Really? Alaska is part of the United States? Not many people my age know that Alaska is part of the United States."

Me (reading from computer): "'Alaska was a Russian colony from 1744 until the United States bought it for $7.2 million in 1867. It was made a state in 1959.'"

Mom: "Hmm…"

Me: "You came to the United States in 1959. Alaska has been a state the entire time you've been here."

Mom: "Whatever."

My Wacky Mom on Puppetry

Mom: "Look at that photo of you. You look so happy. Who took your picture?"

Me: "A woman named Eyoalha Baker took pictures of me and a whole bunch of other people jumping. She calls it the 'Jump for Joy Photo Project.'"

Mom: "Where did she take your picture?"

Me: "In front of a house in Palm Springs with a really cool pink door! I wanted to jump in front of the door wearing a pink polka-dotted dress."

Mom: "You actually jumped?"

Me: "What do you think?"

Mom: "I thought they put strings on you, like a puppet."

My Wacky Mom on "Oriental People"

Mom: "I met with a lady to see if I could get a helper. She's a big, fat lady. She's nice."

Me: "So, what did she say?"

Mom: "Yes. She said I could have a helper for three hours a week. The lady asked if I wanted an Oriental person to help me. I told her, 'No way! Oriental people are a pain in the butt.'"

Me: "You actually said that?!"

Mom: "Oriental people are busybodies. I told her I wanted an American."

Me: "Are you saying that you are a pain in the butt?"

Mom: "Yes. I know I'm a pain in the butt. I'm too much. I know how it is..."

My Wacky Mom on Social Media

YouTube: Subscribe to the MyWackyMom channel

Facebook: Like MyWackyMom

Twitter: Follow @My_Wacky_Mom

Instagram: Follow My_Wacky_Mom

Check out MyWackyMom.com and email *YOUR* wacky mom stories, photos, and videos to
kimiko@MyWackyMom.com

We would love to hear from you!
Domo arigato!

Credits

Front Cover: Use of Girl Scout uniform courtesy Girl Scouts of the USA.

Figure 15 (On Male News Anchors). Created by Christopher D. Mott, 2019.

Figure 17(On Love Triangles). "Old Couple (2)" by Ichiban Yada is licensed under CC-BY-4.0

Figure 19(On How to 'Do Sex'). "Couple in Love," Created 4 July 2017, licensed under CCO-1.0

Figure 21(On Keith Urban). "Keith Urban in PoAH.JPG" by J-smith.17. Created 4 November 2007, licensed under CC BY-SA 3.0

Page 32 "Fly, Eagles Fly (Pep Band Fight Song)". Philadelphia Eagles. 2019. Retrieved 2019-07-25.

Figure 41(On Roku). "Racoon @ Stanley Park (7338309360).jpg" by Go ToVan. Created 3 June 2012, licensed under CC BY 2.0

Figure 43(On Jerry Springer). "Silhouette of a dancer on a pole" by Momoko. Created 9 December 2012, licensed under CCO-1.0

Figure 49(On Phone Sex). "Male Cartoon Semen Comic Happy Sperm Green" on Max Pixel, licensed under CCO-1.0

Figure 57(On Vanity). "Wig Shop Heads Mannequins" by Mike Mozart. Created 2015 February 6, licensed under CC BY 2.0

Figure 63(On the 600-Year-Old Pope). "Friar-pope-old-stick-nostalgia-3633251" by Gianni Crestani. Created 2018 August 2, licensed under CCO-1.0.

Figure 65(On Helping Her Helper). Created by Christopher D. Mott, 2019.

Figure 73(On Watching Parades). "SF Pride Drag Queens.jpg" by Pretzelpaws. Created 2005 June 26, licensed under CC BY-SA 3.0

Figure 89(On Forgiveness). "Forgiveness-sand-summer-send-beach-1767432" by BenteBoe is licensed under CCO-1.0

Figure 91(On Random Acts of Kindness). Created by Christopher D. Mott, 2019

Figure 101(On the 100-Year-Old Cat). "pxhere.com/en/photo/53160" on pxhere.com. Created 2016 December 28, licensed under CC BY-SA 2.0.

Figure 103(On Grocery Shopping). "hard-labour-sacks-transportation-285215/" by pucho. Created 2011 February 25, licensed under CCO-1.0.

Figure 129(On Batman). "Gotham City Saviour (2430422227).jpg" by Syed Abdul Kaliq. Created 2008 April 18, licensed by CC BY 2.0.

Figure 131(On Getting to the Mechanic). "plumber-repair-mechanic-plumbing-35611/" on Pixabay. Created 2012 April 16, licensed under CCO-1.0.

Figure 139(On "Bookstore Kimi-chan"). "Scary-girl-crazy-knife-unpleasant-650295" on Pixabay. Created 2015 February 25, licensed under CCO-1.0

"Motherhood: All love begins and ends there."

- Robert Browning (poet, 1812 - 1889)

65017221R00084

Made in the USA
Middletown, DE
02 September 2019